For more information about special discounts for bulk orders, email:
info@howangelsaremade.com

ISBN (Hardcover): 978-1-7350238-0-9
ISBN (Paperback): 978-1-7350238-1-6
ISBN (E-Book): 978-1-7350238-4-7

First Edition, 2020

Learn more about our story at www.HowAngelsAreMade.com
Tag us on Instagram and Facebook @HowAngelsAreMade
Use Hashtag: #HowAngelsAreMade

How Angels Are Made

A Journey of Love, Grief, and Understanding Through the Eyes of a Child

By: Bryson Thompson Sr.

Dedication

To BJ,
Your Grandmother loved you from the bottom of her heart. Every time she saw you, she had the biggest smile and loved spoiling her grandbaby. Never forget her unconditional love for you and I know she would want you to share that same love with others you come in contact with. She'll be watching over you forever.

Malcolm and Maya,
You never had a chance to meet your Grandma Gwen but I see her spirit in both of you daily. Although she is not here to meet you, her love for you is as big as the moon. All of you are her special projects from heaven and she's watching over you throughout your entire life.

Pops, Tike, and Shaquille,
Fellas, it was a tough loss and I'm sure you still feel the pain like me but I know momma is proud of each and every one of us. Let's continue to honor and expand the legacy she has left for us.

My beautiful wife,
Momma loved you like a daughter and was always proud of you. I see her influence in how you interact with our children and I appreciate your support through our times of pain. I love you and hope you know that your spirit is what she always prayed for in our family.

This book belongs to

BJ was busy getting ready for bed.

“Get your pajamas on and I’ll read you your favorite book," said Mommy.

After changing, he curled up next to his mother on his bed. As they got ready to read, his mother noticed a curious look on her son’s face.

“What’s the matter, baby boy?” she asked.

"Mommy," said BJ. "Where do ANGELS come from?”

“Well, son, ANGELS are very special people who have left Earth and watch over special little boys from a place we call Heaven,” Mommy answered.

“Awesome!” exclaimed BJ “Do you think I’ll ever have an angel one day!”

"I'm sure you will one day, my dear, I'm sure you will," said Mommy before opening the book and beginning to read.

The next morning, BJ woke up to the sound of a car pulling into the driveway. He leapt out of bed and ran downstairs to see one of his favorite people standing at the door.

"GRANDMA!" BJ shouted excitedly, running towards her with arms open for a big hug.

"Hey, Grandma's man!" beamed Grandma, wrapping her arms around her little grandson.

"How are you today?" asked BJ, looking up at her.

“Doing fine,” answered Grandma with an expression she often used.

But there was something different about Grandma today. It was something BJ couldn’t quite put his finger on.

“Come and let me show you my new games Grandma,” encouraged BJ, dragging Grandma over to the play area where they spent the afternoon playing together.

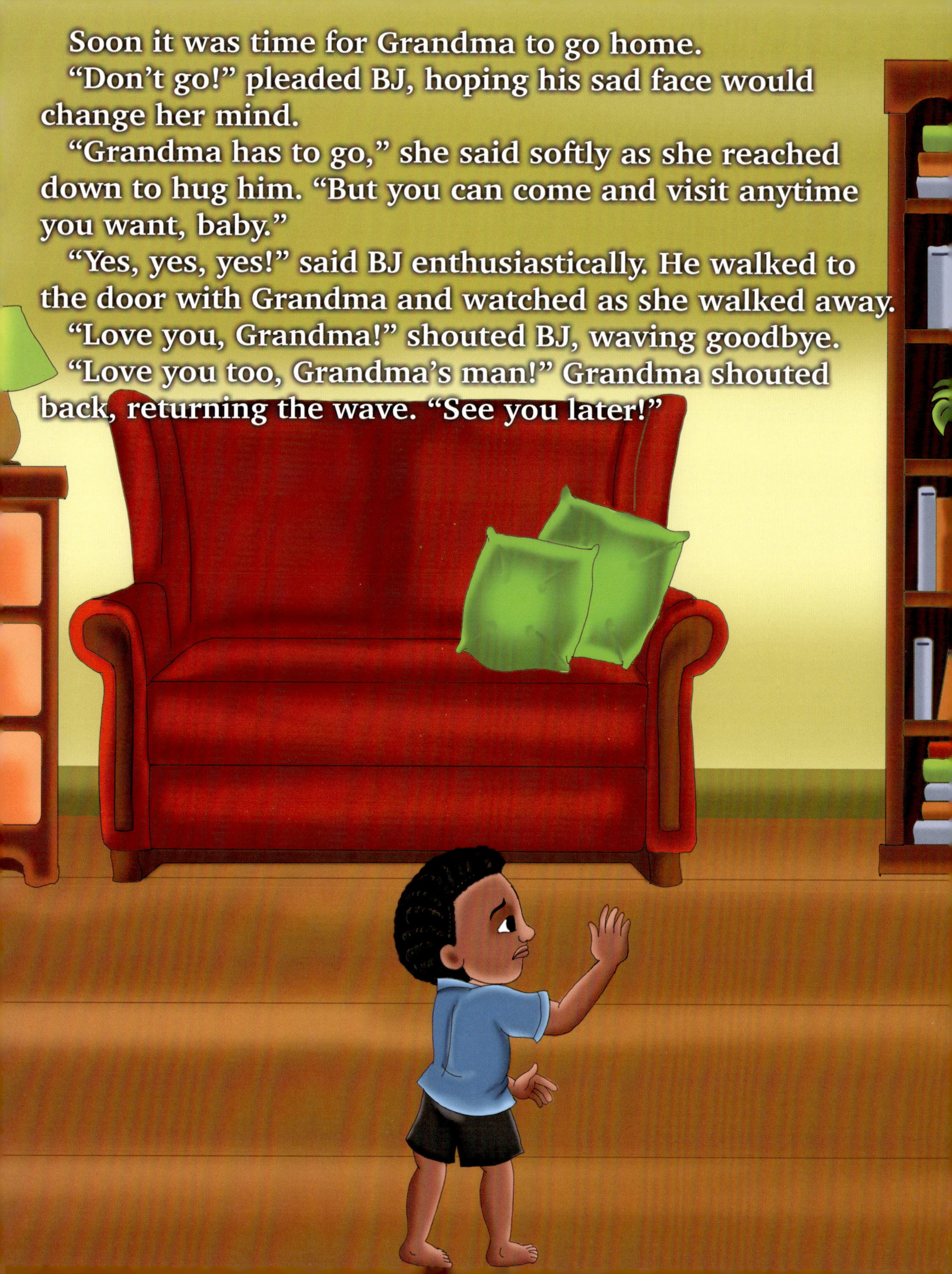

Soon it was time for Grandma to go home.

"Don't go!" pleaded BJ, hoping his sad face would change her mind.

"Grandma has to go," she said softly as she reached down to hug him. "But you can come and visit anytime you want, baby."

"Yes, yes, yes!" said BJ enthusiastically. He walked to the door with Grandma and watched as she walked away.

"Love you, Grandma!" shouted BJ, waving goodbye.

"Love you too, Grandma's man!" Grandma shouted back, returning the wave. "See you later!"

A week later, BJ called Grandma, a routine they both looked forward to.

"How are you, Grandma?" he asked.

"Doing fine," replied Grandma. "Are you being a good boy at school?"

"Yes, I am," said BJ, secretly hoping that Daddy hadn't told her about his day at school.

Grandma encouragingly said, "Always go to school, listen to the teacher, and learn your lessons. Then you will grow up to be a great young man who helps other people."

"OK," replied BJ, taking the advice to heart. "Love you, Grandma!"

"Where are we going, Daddy?" asked BJ from the back of the car.

"Grandma's house to check on her," said Daddy.

"GRANDMA'S HOUSE!" BJ yelled as he saw a very familiar house.

He ran through the door to be greeted by the biggest smile.

“How’s Grandma’s man?” said Grandma, embracing him in a warm hug.

“I’m doing great, Grandma!” said BJ, always happy to see his grandma. “How about you?”

A brief second passed before Grandma responded, “Doing fine.” Soon she was following behind BJ to the kitchen where she always had the best food. As they walked, BJ couldn’t help but notice Grandma was moving a step slower than normal.

His concerns were quickly washed away when he and Grandma spent the rest of the day doing all the things they loved doing together. Grandma showed him how to make cookies. They sang songs from Grandma's phone. They talked about school, friends, and watched some of their favorite TV shows.

Soon it was time to go home. While Daddy was loading up the car, BJ ran back into the house to get another special hug from Grandma.

"Love you, Grandma," said BJ, squeezing tight.

"Love you too, little man," replied Grandma. She finally letting go as Daddy gestured for BJ to go. "See you later!"

"See you later!" said BJ. As the car pulled away, BJ continued waving as his grandma grew smaller and smaller.

Several weeks later, BJ entered his parent's room to see Daddy packing his suitcase.

"Where are we going, Daddy?" BJ asked.

Daddy turned around and BJ could see his eyes were wet from tears. "We have to go to Grandma's house," he said. His voice was shaking.

"What's wrong, Daddy?" asked BJ, concerned because his Daddy never normally cried.

"We got some bad news today, baby boy," answered Daddy. "We have to go to Grandma's house, so we are getting ready."

On the way to Grandma's house, Daddy and Mommy explained to BJ that Grandma had a bad disease called stomach cancer and she was gone to a better place.

Once they got there, BJ noticed several cars parked out the front, instantly recognizing them as belonging to his uncles.

Before his parents could stop him, BJ ran up to the house, through the door and his eyes scanned the room for his favorite person.

“Where’s Grandma?” he asked aloud, looking around the house without a sighting of her.

“Grandma’s not here, buddy. Come sit beside me and Mommy.” Daddy said, placing BJ between both of them. “Remember when we talked about Grandma being gone to a better place?”

"At some point, all of us eventually die, leave earth and move to God's house where we become angels," said Daddy, choking back tears.

“Will I be able to see her again?” asked BJ, wanting one of Grandma’s big hugs now more than ever.

“Where she’s gone, you won’t be able to see her," said Mommy. "But she's always smiling, looking down at you and making sure you're safe. Whenever you feel scared or sad, think about Grandma, and she will help you feel better.”

A few days later, BJ and Daddy walked up to a large white church. Inside the church, BJ spotted a familiar face lying in a beautiful grey box.

“Is Grandma OK?” asked BJ, wondering if she was sleeping.

"Yes, she's more than fine," said Daddy, wiping his eyes. "She's become an angel and angels don't need their old bodies."

“Will she still look like Grandma?” asked BJ

“She will look exactly like you remembered her,” replied Daddy. “She’s looking down at you from God’s house.”

BJ held on tightly to his father and looked at his Grandma as she lay still in front of him.

"Love you, Grandma," said BJ as he blew her a final kiss.

As BJ got himself ready for bed, he found himself thinking about God's house. "Mommy?" asked BJ "Where is God's house and what is Grandma doing there?"

"It's in Heaven, up there in the sky," Mommy said as she looked out the window. "Your Grandma is a very special person. Now that she's in Heaven, she can be your special guardian angel."

BJ looked down at the toy in his lap. It was a gift Grandma had gotten him last Christmas. He remembered unwrapping and playing with it. It made him wonder how Grandma was doing in Heaven. Suddenly, he heard Grandma's voice saying, "Doing fine." It was as if she was in the room with them.

“She’s looking out for us right now, isn’t she, Mommy?” asked BJ.

“Yes, she is, my love. We have our angel protecting us.” replied Mommy with a slight smile.

Feeling happy with that thought, BJ looked up at the ceiling…

...imagining Grandma looking down at him from the heavens.

Although you may lose someone in their physical form, their memories and lessons live forever. Through your life and greatness, they will remain! You are a living testimony to their legacy and they will continue to watch down over you.

In memory of Gwendolyn J. Tanner May 2, 1958 - Feb 3, 2016.

Dear Momma,

What can I say? You were a legend and a queen to me. It's been years since I saw your wonderful smile and had the opportunity to give you a big hug. Your love, however, is still present in my life more than ever. My only goal was to make you proud and I know that goal was accomplished a long time ago, because you loved all of us unconditionally. My goal now is to have half of the faith and character that guided you on a daily basis. You were the originator of a service based life, as you always put the needs of others over your own. You sacrificed for the greater good of the family and made sure you took care of those you loved. Thank you for being that much needed role model. I'll never forget that!

Speaking of legacy, I wish you were here to laugh at your wild grandbabies (I know you would fuss at me for calling them wild, but it's the truth). My apologies if I was as wild as young BJ, who still misses you till this day. He is as active as ever and smart, as you probably already know. We're still working on his behavior, but he is a Thompson (shoulder shrug). I'm sure you've been watching your little Boss Baby Malcolm grow up. He is as bright as they come and light years ahead of his time. We swear he's been here before and you must have given him the game plan. Lastly, I know you've been smiling ear to ear with the introduction of young Maya in the world. She is a spitting image of you and everything we were hoping for in a baby girl. Don't worry about the spoiling, Mr. and Mrs. Mac got her in that department! We will make sure the kids always keep your memory alive and know how instrumental you were in laying the foundation for our family. Thanks for being our leader!

Lastly, all of your boys are standing strong. Pops is still a champion and keeping us all together. I know you are proud of him and he's keeping his new yellow toy clean under his shed! Shaquille and Tike are still making moves and carrying on your legacy. I know you are as proud of them as I am. Your girl, Tricey, is doing her thing too. She's been taking care of the kids like a champ and she's even tried to learn a couple of new things in the kitchen. I know she learned a ton from the time you both shared together. As for me, I'm still into a little of everything. I can't stay still from trying to reach my crazy goals and be the person you raised me to be. I still miss you daily and I swear to keep your legacy alive as long as I can breathe. I can't thank you enough for all that you done for me and I love you forever. Good bye for now, tell Granny I said "hey" and I can't wait to see you on the other side.

Love you

B

About the Author
Bryson Thompson Sr.

Bryson Thompson is from a small town called Little Africa, South Carolina. He is a proud husband, father, educator, mentor, entrepreneur, and author. With 10+ years of experience as a special educator and mental health professional, Bryson dedicated his life to finding ways to uplift young men and women. He is formally trained with a bachelor's in special education from Clemson University and Masters in Behavior / Learning Disabilities from Georgia State University. He works continually to find ways to enhance the lives and experiences of the future generation.

After losing his mother to stomach cancer in 2016, Bryson was able to transform his pain into his first book "How Angels are Made."

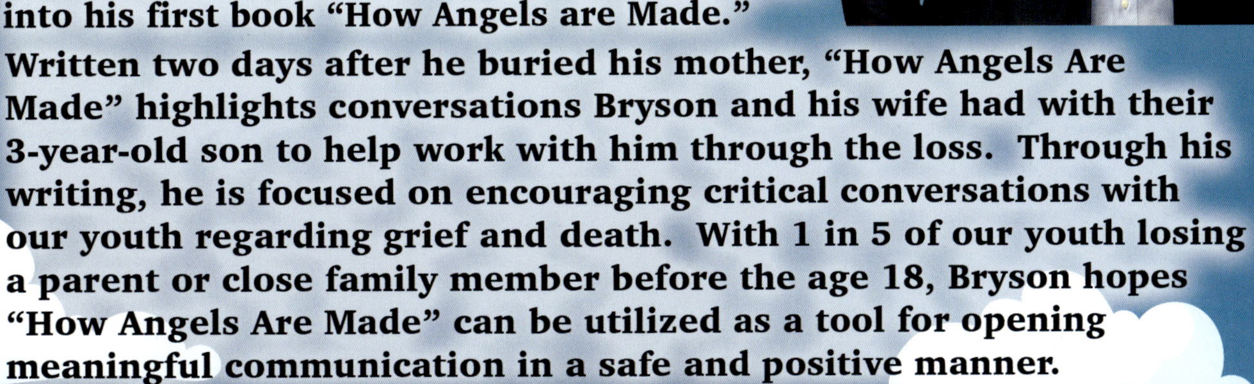

Written two days after he buried his mother, "How Angels Are Made" highlights conversations Bryson and his wife had with their 3-year-old son to help work with him through the loss. Through his writing, he is focused on encouraging critical conversations with our youth regarding grief and death. With 1 in 5 of our youth losing a parent or close family member before the age 18, Bryson hopes "How Angels Are Made" can be utilized as a tool for opening meaningful communication in a safe and positive manner.

For more information on the book,
visit www.HowAngelsAreMade.com